# Kitchen Apocrypha

# Kitchen
# APOCRYPHA

POEMS

BY

~~Gregory Emilio~~

*Greg Emilio* (signature)

ABLE MUSE PRESS

For Missy + Jeff. Thank you for reading!
With friendship, hunger, + love!

— G

# Able Muse Press

www.ablemusepress.com

Library of Congress Cataloging-in-Publication Data

Names: Emilio, Gregory, 1987- author.
Title: Kitchen apocrypha / poems by Gregory Emilio.
Description: San Jose, CA : Able Muse Press, 2022.
Identifiers: LCCN 2021060276 (print) | LCCN 2021060277 (ebook) | ISBN
   9781773491707 (hardcover) | ISBN 9781773491080 (paperback) | ISBN
   9781773491073 (ebook)
Subjects: LCGFT: Poetry.
Classification: LCC PS3605.M524 K58 2022 (print) | LCC PS3605.M524
   (ebook) | DDC 811/.6--dc23/eng/20211213
LC record available at https://lccn.loc.gov/2021060276
LC ebook record available at https://lccn.loc.gov/2021060277


Printed in the United States of America

Cover image: *Kitchen Help* by Isidor Kaufmann

Cover & book design by Alexander Pepple

Able Muse Press is an imprint of *Able Muse: A Review of Poetry, Prose & Art*—
   at www.ablemuse.com

Able Muse Press
467 Saratoga Avenue #602
San Jose, CA 95129

There is a communion of more than our bodies
when bread is broken and wine drunk.
— M. F. K. Fisher


I had been hungry, all the Years—
— Emily Dickinson

# *Acknowledgments*

Grateful acknowledgment is made to the editors of the following publications in which these poems, or earlier versions, first appeared:

*Able Muse*: "Diminishing Sestina"

*Best New Poets 2018*: "High on the Hog"

*Blue River*: "Travel Notes: Mykonos"

*Cumberland River Review*: "Mushrooms in a Tennessee Graveyard" and "Saint Prodigal"

*Foothill*: "Meeting *la Matriarca*"

*F(r)iction*: "First Food"

*Gastronomica*: "Miracle in a Time of Dregs"

*Green Briar Review*: "A Farmers Market in Georgia," "My Mother and My Father in the Kitchen," and "Whetstone Sapphics"

*Letters*: "Saying Grace in a Time of Drought"

*Mid-American Review*: "Meditation at Waffle House"

*Midwestern Gothic*: "Last Shift at the Purple Turtle"

*Miramar*: "Corazón de Tierra"

*Muse/A*: "The Amateur Cook and His Lover" and "Unabashed Sapphics on Hot and Heavy"

*Nashville Review*: "Saying Grace in a Time of Too Much (Elegy for a Future Loss)"

*North American Review*: "Grits (and Love and Happiness)," "Hymn to Fennel (*Máratho*)," and "Prayer to Garlic"

*[PANK]*: "*Omophagia*"

*Permafrost*: "Reckoning"

*Profane*: "Elegy for Barbecue"

*The Reach of Song*: "The Book of Salt" and "For Everything in Paradise"

*Rock & Sling*: "Butter Thief"

*Southern Humanities Review*: "After the Last Supper"

*Spoon River Poetry Review*: "Bethesda" and "Whenever You Eat This"

*Tahoma Literary Review*: "Renunciation"

*The Poet's Billow*: "A Lesson in Hunger"

*The Ekphrastic Review*: "Varieties of Communion"

*Tinderbox Poetry Journal*: "Jesus as a Jaded Lover" and "*Sparagmos*"

*The Windhover*: "Saying Grace (Without Grace)"

*Unbroken*: "Quitting"

*Valparaiso Poetry Review*: "Rapture"


"A Lesson in Hunger" was among a sequence of poems that won the 2015 Pangaea Prize from the Poet's Billow.

"First Food" won *F(r)iction*'s 2018 Summer Poetry Contest.

"For Everything in Paradise" won Georgia Poetry Society's 2019 Byron Herbert Reece Prize.

"Japanese Maple" won White Oak Kitchen's 2020 Prize for Southern Poetry.

# Contents

# Kitchen Apocrypha

## II

## III

# Kitchen Apocrypha

# Rapture

A sudden rush: the blade buried halfway
into an onion, the chopping block left
in medias res, garlic cloves cleft,
unminced beside glasses of cabernet.

Stove flames lap blue the bottom of a pot,
and the water rolls in a steady boil
like the earth's molten core, or soil
wasted in a field of squash gone to rot.

Will any sight be stranger than a kitchen
emptied of its humans? No naked eyes
to water, or hands to hold the knives.
None to feel the flames. Bereft of heaven,

we stumbled out of the bedroom, dizzy
and undone, rapt and abandoned: hungry.

I

# Prayer to Garlic

*Eat no onions nor garlic, for we are to utter sweet breath . . .*
— A Midsummer Night's Dream, *Shakespeare*

Stinking rose, bulbous bride of the rough earth,
come up you coy, cloistered, dirt-bound moon,
slip from your skin and give us the hot tongue,
bitter-sticking syllables to haunt our breath
like the parched voices of the dead, consumed
by wildfire, sprung up, gunned down, got and gone.
Gilroy galled, garish, *gar*, you're named a leek's
spear, and I'm guilty for turning too soon
to doom. Cloven goddess, weird allium,
if we can't savor your slow-roasted sweet,
we're done.

# The Book of Salt

Not a woman turned into a pillar
of mineral devotion, a mirror
of a million diminutive crystals
glancing back at the burning world.
Not the satisfyingly thick pinch
of kosher flakes raining from fingers
into a pot of boiling pasta water.
Not the pink curing salt massaged
into the fat cap of a Boston Butt.
Not the first clumsy grains we gathered
like manna from the evaporating sea.
Not Solnitsata, the first city in Europe.
Not the wondrous failure of California's
Salton Sea. Not saltines. Not the Hebrew
covenant of salt with God, not Romans
salting crops after they sacked Carthage.
Not Gandhi's salt *satyagraha*, dull
diamond of daily life as the symbol
to resist the British *raj*. Not the salt
swimming in our blood, on our tongues—
not the sweat of a lover's neck. Not *fleur
de sel*, Maldon, *sel gris*, or Himalayan
pink. Not the iodized, not icy roads,
not traded for gold, or buried with kings
in Egyptian tombs. Not camouflaged
in *kombu* or *miso*, or sprinkled
down the brown neck of a Pacifico.
Not laughingly thrown over the shoulder.
Not saying someone's "worth their salt."
Not salt. Not salt but a dying man
and the sulfuric, microbe-rich rust
of a slot canyon in Nevada, a chasm

along the Colorado where geothermal
pools burbled over a hundred degrees,
where the arid August air rolled at one
hundred and fifteen, and this mirage
of a man loitered near our kayaks,
lapping up unfiltered river brine
from a scavenged piece of Tupperware.
He babbled about mushrooms, the sun,
his face streaked with creeks of blood—
all pink flesh except for a small towel.
We shooed him away from our camp
and he spent all night floating in the hot
springs, moaning among coyote kills,
the salt raising up his rabid body
into a Mojave sky racked with stars.
Not a bruise-black tablecloth spangled
with a shaker's uncountable specks.
Not the nervous jokes about him
as we cooked our fish, not the fear
that he'd slit our throats while we slept.
Not the moon drifting over the earth
like a chipped dinner plate. Not the last
of our supplies, the dried peach halves
we gave him after he shook us awake
in the morning, his shoulders glowing
with an ash-white scrim. Not an angel
from Revelation or Rilke. Not a man
not worth his salt. Not salt but the way
we turned away, lugged our kayaks back
down the shore with a promise to send help
and paddled home. Not our desert sins,
and not forgiveness. Not left like teeth,
or the soul's crystalline grit. Not God.
Just the taste, so bright and indifferent.

## Saying Grace

As a child I moaned
pure empty preamble
impatiently *God is good*
but *let us* now cooking
*for our* dear *food* Lord
more than just *amen*
under the weight
for the cow we killed
the butter of its milk
*amen* the blank gut
of the all-consuming
as a cheap *amen* gone
like grapes raised
let's talk to God
*by* the bittersweet root
kneading the cosmic
too much I mean *amen*
our gathering hunger
the sacral tongue
*our daily* dying

## (Without Grace)

*God*
*is great* as we held hands
passing the breadbasket
on our own *thank him*
and let it mean so much
let us bow and bruise
of so much praise
and the tufts of grass
and the vacant sky
that begat the all
all and us graceless
to a better place
on crystal stems
as if we're buried
of prayer *his hands*
meat *we all are fed*
and *give us* now
the vulture's wings
to circle *Lord* to sing
*bread*

# Hymn to Fennel (*Máratho*)

*According to legend, an Athenian messenger was sent from Marathon
to Athens, a distance of about 25 miles (40 km), and there he
announced the Persian defeat before dying of exhaustion.*
— Encyclopedia Britannica

Praise this bone-white bulb of the ancient landscape,
glaucous green stalks and dill-like fronds flickering
ad infinitum, like the myths that seemed to
spring up overnight,

rampant as weeds. Praise roasting to bring out its
sweetness, wedges caramelized in the oven,
pile of ribs anointed with oil, the kitchen
aromatic as

Delphi's oracle, the belly of prophecy.
Praise the raw slices shaved on a mandoline,
vegetal bitterness bright as a honed blade,
ready to take your

finger's pink tip. People forget it was a
hollow stalk of giant fennel that carried
fire from Olympus, the root of all our art
hidden in a root

vegetable. Praise for the liver gutted
every day. Praise the flavor of Italian
sausage. Praise absinthe and the latest foodie
trends. People forget

*marathon* comes from the Greek word for fennel,
name of the place where it ran wild, where thousands
died in the flowing hills. Praise fire. Praise how we
run across the earth.

# The Weariness of Risotto

Pearls of arborio sloughing off starch
in a ceaseless cycle of stock and stir,
I keep the steady rhythm of the simmer,
letting the black-bottomed pot almost parch

before ladling more saffron-blossomed
broth, the steam immediate and lush,
answering the spatula's repetitive push
and mirrored pull, swiveling the softened

mass of grains in drunken figure eights,
a mushy gesture toward the infinite—
an ad hoc attempt to get intimate
with the life that heat evaporates,

the essence of chicken bones spirited
away, ascending scents, leaving behind
a trace in the grain, ghost given blind
to some higher purpose. I intend

to learn this dish by heart, to skip Google
searches, and muscle-remember that rice
transcends by breaking down, paradise
rendered and reduced to the beautiful

curse of our relentless need to eat.
Creamy, mumbling, a bowl of risotto
tells us that maybe all we ever know
is weariness. So be it. *Bon appétit.*

# Mushrooms in a Tennessee Graveyard

For a moment, I'm tempted to believe
that the pumpkin-colored constellations
of chanterelles blossomed above a grave
possess in their ribbed, wavering tunics
and scalloped ridges, in their apricot scent,
some mineral trace of the long-gone bodies
below them, some fecund, far-off echo—
a little human afterlife in the spores.

After a hard rain, anything remains
possible. Even the moist, cricketed idea
of the divine, a bright fungal miracle.
Elizabeth Anne Riley's bone dust rising
up delicious, in spangled profusion—
an offering to eat, if not believe.

# Chicken of the Woods

*For Hudson Holly, Nantahala National Forest, North Carolina*

We find them flaming, fatty, licked with dew
on a desiccated stump. Surreal choice
edible, its yellow-orange brackets
bursting the coffin oak. *Sulphur shelf.*
A decomposer fungus that breaks
down lignin with the right amount
of warmth and rain. Contingent ember
edges, a glistening link in the ongoing
feast of living things.
                    Discovering it
just so in the middle of my life, mastered
by an Appalachian column of light,
I get on my knees, and take out my knife.

\*      \*      \*

Beside a drowsy fire of damp twigs,
bellies waxing with the hefty slivers of this
butter-bathed polypore, this peculiar god-
send, foraged boon, we talk of the recent
bear encounters in these woods, thefts
of hung food, black muzzles nudging
mesh tent walls.
                Then we hear a small
creature—anonymous rodent or rabbit—
shrieking for its life. Once, twice, high-
pitched, bone-bright.
                  Then the thunder-
clap of an owl in full-throated thrall.

\*      \*      \*

All night long, a legion of fungi rises up
in the moonlight, donning their hoods,
whispering to root systems in a language
of sugar and phosphorus.
                    Look at us
lying here listening to every leafy shiver,
to the green rustlings of lurkers
poking around our camp. Our fingers
tightening around our pocketknives
while our plates are licked clean.

# Elegy for Barbecue

At J. D. Boone's, a ramshackle palace
of smoke and pork, the college kids
recite the mantra of *low and slow*,
study the way bark blackens on a slab
of brisket after ten hours in the feverish
belly of Big Mama, a red behemoth
of steel and heat. They learn to love
flesh that falls apart in the mouth,
food that sends them toward the primitive
worship of oak, perpetual embers,
the melting fat on a rack of ribs.
Unctuous animal smoke penetrates
hair, fingernails, lingers along
arms like a sunburn. They wear
T-shirts that exclaim, *You can't beat
our meat!* and take turns smoking
an apple pipe in the walk-in freezer,
then rubbing their torsos together,
smacking their lips in communion
as if customers, thesis statements,
student loan debt all ceased to exist—
such revelations as they straddle
bags of frozen bones. *Cooking makes
us human*, they chorus, anointing pork
butts with dry rub before hoisting them
up onto Big Mama's carbon-black racks.
*Dudes, the afterlife's nothing but a rumor*,
they whisper, post-shift, passing a bottle
of bourbon back and forth. After, they take
to the buzzing streets of San Luis Obispo

by bike or board, handing out corn bread
to the homeless, to their favorite bouncers.
They want to spread this gospel
of the feast forever. But they will
graduate, move on, and these years
of faith in the ability of barbecue
to save them will fade, like the fire
after the nights they got too wasted
to remember to load the wood.

# High on the Hog

Means blessed, profligate, blind.
Means the pigs on which we live
live in obscene packed pens or fairy-tale
pasturelands. They taste better when
they die happy, the butcher on TV said.
Means fatback, slab bacon, means bellies
and butts, means pancetta, prosciutto.
Means lick your chops, country ham
and collards, mama's applesauce.
Smoked from the roota to the toota,
nothing of this animal life wasted,
suckling, apple-mouthed on a platter.
Porcine means piggish, pudgy, ugly—
but pigs are also sentient and social
and gassed together hysterical
in abattoirs as big as football fields.
Means the most humane method.
Means not hocks, nor hoofs,
not the lower cuts but higher up
where we ride the hog, we,
the only animals in denial,
self-appointed shepherds
ark-ready to ride this out,
going for broke. Meaning caviar
from Siberia and champagne
from places we can't pronounce.
Means leaving it all on the table,
resplendent. Rotting cornucopias.
Means my grandmother had a poster
above the kitchen table in her trailer

of a man on the hood of a Rolls,
wineglass in his gloved hand,
*POVERTY SUCKS* in bold
below him. Means we all come
from dust if you go back far enough.
Means we made the animals
dance on our tongues, named
them under lock and key, doomed
by taste, that primal superhighway
of pleasure. High on the hog means
I'm eating a ham and cheese croissant
as we speak, does not mean ancient,
necessary spears piercing the side
of a screaming razorback. It means
my grandma feared the big bully pig
on the family farm in Kansas who'd nip
her heels as she sprinted to the outhouse.
Means I've never met any of the pigs
I've eaten. I mean there's plenty,
so take more than what you need
of the fatted, gelatinous dream.
I mean ham-fisted, run amok—
we can't stop because we can't
stop, please get me off this
high horse, this other white
meat we've gotten so high on.
I mean. Dear swine, noble suids,
forgive us. Your meat, your sweet
meat was always more than food.

# Oh, Let's Just Be Hogs: A Cento

Saint Anthony, patron of sausage makers,
guide my pen and unkink my tongue. I sing
of a hog theater where hogs performed as men,
had men been hogs—dolphins of the backyard,
frolickers in the gray and eternal muck, the holy
ones like Christ, who will befriend their destroyers,
whose heaven is the only one worth wanting,
where cue joints rise through smoke and glow,
each tongue ready to map the ramshackle
rib or rump, dry rub or ketchup, bacon,
chitlin, crackling, sin: the eternal terms
of future pork roasts fattened toward
oblivion. But this is not about love.
Once a pig is hung and cut straight,
cut from rectum to neck, step inside
her death like it is a room: that is how
to touch her now. The Lord said, *You must*
*not eat their meat or touch their carcasses.*
Then came the end of the rib. Don't dig
on swine, that's all. But bacon tastes good;
pork chops taste good. The great chain's links
alive and hermetic as bone. From the sweet
glues of the trotters, come the sweet kinks
of the fist. Everything flowers from within,
though sometimes it's necessary to reteach
a thing its loveliness—as Saint Francis
put his hand on the creased forehead
of the sow, and told her in words
and in touch the long, perfect loveliness
of sow. So every word reverberates

and mystery's sown again. *Sooey*
*sooey:* this is how we are civilized.
Hogs streamed out of the theater
crying, only hogs, only hogs.

Sources: Russell Edson, Rodney Jones, Rebecca Gayle Howell, Galway Kinnell, William Matthews, Jake Adam York, Philip Levine, Honoree Fanonn Jeffers, Kevin Young, Leviticus, and Quentin Tarantino.

# A Farmers Market in Georgia

*After Allen Ginsberg's "A Supermarket in California"*

It's spring now and everything is crazy
in bloom—dogwoods, redbuds, pollen
shaking the air like an overheated lover,
and I tumble like a dandelion spore
toward Your Dekalb Farmers Market,
just past the neon dayglow of a strip club,
lured today by the tender shoots of spring
garlic, the reclusive ramps, all the alliums
making me think of dear dead Frank O'Hara
slashing up from the soil like a voice needing
to gab, sun-hungry for black coffee, cigarettes,
a few swigs of Strega—how briskly he coasts
here now in his white-collared shirt, dabs
of chocolate malt dappled on his cuffs—
raw, uprooted, he strolls past the collards
sweating in their bins, the lusty bundles
of basil, past knobs of galangal, trumpet
mushrooms, dragon fruit and durian
poised alien and askew, the air perfumed
with *pasillas, anchos,* and *chiles de árbol,*
and don't get me started on the oblong
avocados growing dreamy green
in their brown husks, or the grandmas
sniffing strawberries for the stained lips
of childhood—we're all here, you, me,
Frank, and you, and you too, all of us
present in this vegetal landscape
of food harvested by human hands,

and my burlap sacks are bulging
but feasible, and a woman with lilac
bags under her eyes whose name tag
says she speaks Farsi and Aramaic,
whose hijab is bright as a chive blossom,
hums PLUs as she rings up my fruit,
and when she hands me my change
our fingers touch—swift as onionskin—
and I whisper *thanks* and she nods
toward the exit: Frank fading into
the light with a handful of figs.

# Southern *Xenia*

June once again in this state famous
for its peaches and so-called southern
hospitality, season of seersucker clichés
and days riven by freight trains of rain.
Another June and I'm in love with *y'all*,
the word wafting like browned butter,
yawning vocable making the air itself
more hospitable. Forgive a California
son his wonderment at southern tongues:
my first taste of legit pimento cheese
was damn near religious epiphany.
I came here a stranger but found kin
in kitchens and dish pits, in battered
skillets and broken shaker tins, faith
in food service as a reliable way of life.

Hospitality was ritual in ancient Greece:
any stranger greeted with food, shelter,
a bath, no questions asked until the basics
had been provided. Part of it was fear that
Zeus might be wearing a beggar's mask,
might sow ruin thick as kudzu on your house
if you shut the door too fast. This June a face
mask muffles my voice and hides my smile
when I talk to tables. They have no idea who
I might be beneath, but most of them know
the most infamous case of improper *xenia*.
Paris was a guest in Menelaus's house—
slipped with his wife out the back door.

But this isn't Sparta. Here in Atlanta,
restaurants are just opening back up,
and I greet each guest as if something
hiding in their bodies might kill me.
Ahmaud Arbery also lived in this state
famous for its hospitality. Forgive me
for falling for words like a day-tripper
on a train, the passing landscape framed
impossibly lush. Tonight, we closed early
in fear of protests. The Latin root *hospes*
can mean either stranger, host, or guest:
the door held open for *y'all* becomes us,
another June dripping down our chins.

## Meditation at Waffle House

I find it here among the griddle's chatter,
the expo passing the baton of orders
in swift lingo through the sizzling air
to the "Rockstar Grill Operator"—*Marty,*
*drop one bacon, three hash brown, one scattered,*
*two smothered and covered, and two eggs triple*
*scrambled*—praise in the music of cooking,
in the clatter of steaming silver shaken
to dry, in the cadence of coffee pulled up
on the tongue, the whisper of Tammy's
blue butterfly tattoo and her paper hat,
and even in the manager's garish
"Meat Lover's Waffle Stack Special,"
and the black-and-white photograph of Lucy
who served a superhuman forty-seven years
amid this greasy din, lingua franca
of "Good Food Fast," the irons gaping,
splattered with batter. Walking again
in the rubber tread of nonslip sneakers,
the weary two-step of food service, I think
of all the times I asked, *How was everything?*
only to hear the guest, so eager for low-
hanging fruit, blurt out, *Terrible!* (a fat
grin hovering above their empty plate)
and I'd have to find the inner blank slate,
the peace-that-passes smile because people
should be forgiven for the dumb things
a full belly makes them say. And now
a homeless guy is getting shaken down
by a cop in the parking lot, the black tools

of the cop's belt shaking off the morning
light the way oil slicks send back the sky,
and Shyanne says, *What the hell, Jerry ain't
botherin' nobody*. And in her words I hear
a thing like love lost in the thunderous blue
of the cop's broad back. And in the handcuffs
coming out, breaking bright as a migraine,
I find the American imperative not
to praise, but to keep busy, to beat
the golden yolks until one fine morning.

# Last Shift at the Purple Turtle

Paraplegic, her body beginning to switch
off, major organs first, then cell by cell,
like the windows of a building as night
wears on, Linda hulked in her bed, shook
every so often by the misfiring of her
trigger-happy nervous system, her thick
skin rumbling like the earth's crust along
a shearing fault. She'd apologize, blink
her eyes—a color I can't recall because
I was young and afraid to look. The air
was thick with unguents, egg-like smells
of the sick. Linda spoke as if she was in
another room, her voice carrying down
the long hallway of our shared blood.

&ast;

A catheter bag the color of apricot jam
hung under her bed, and light, loosened
by dusk, slanted through the window,
draping her like a shawl. But my mind
wandered: the night before, a woman
who was wild, freckle-eyed, beautiful,
had snuck onto the stage of the Fox
in downtown Pomona after closing
to sing "Ave Maria" while I sat way up
in the mezzanine, punch-drunk on her
mezzo-soprano until a security guard
gingerly plucked me from my seat.

*

Then again, I *was* in Linda's room,
but she was lying in a cornfield in 1971
just outside of Sioux Falls, South Dakota,
after her last shift at the Purple Turtle,
a dive where the girls wore purple skirts,
where heartland men would drink, crescents
of axle grease under their fingernails, bluish
semicircles under their eyes. This is about
Linda lying along Skunk Creek Road,
nineteen years old, her hair surrounding her
like a headdress, skirt scrunched up
in the dirt, her two little boys crying
as her boyfriend hot-wired a tractor
to drive back to town for help.
Their '42 Ford sputtered and smoked
in a ditch while constellations shone whole,
so unlike the astral grit of Los Angeles.

*

Months before, after the San Fernando
Quake had crumbled freeway overpasses,
Linda had a prophecy on blotter acid
and bad vibes and believed that California
would break off and float into the Pacific
like a slice of cake in a sink of dishwater.
Now here she was, young, pretty, rooted
between yellowed cornstalks, paralyzed
in a half-harvested field. Back in Linda's
room, by her bed, I shifted in my seat,

certain that my life had been too easy,
not the stuff of documentaries. Another
convulsion balled her body up, wrung
her out like a sponge. Slackened light
clung to the windowsill like dust.

\*

A few days ago, the same light, she'd
thought, *this is it*: final levity, the soul
unmooring from the body, rising, free.
She was "goddamn disappointed"
to wake up hours later on her back,
the ceiling gone black, the tidal hum
of the highway ebbing into the room
like water across her skin. Her eyes
held me: how little I knew of the fields
of Sioux Falls, of the weightless moment
when a truck flips, of shielding your kids
as you fly out the window, the dead weight
of a pickup pivoting on your neck the way
she turned on the ball of her foot to shout
*Last call* to the few lugs left at the bar.

\*

How meaningless the ghost of the girl
crooning in Latin to Mother Mary
on the stage of last night's dream,
my suburban triumphs and minor
failures of heart. All these years later,
I want to step back into that room,

to grip my shoulder, lift myself up
and force my gaze into the daylight
of her eyes, then lay my hands upon
her body, and brace for the big one.

# Whetstone Sapphics

Scrape and drag the blade and the whetstone sings its
only song, the rasp of the dead, the dying
cackle, fading breath like a candle calling,
*Wait, there's still light here*—

Back and forth, the shucking of iron atoms,
wheezing, giving, grinding to nothing. Listen:
mountains whittled down by the wind, the ocean
gnawing a cliff like

gnarly bread, the tongue of a cat: your salty
skin. Forgive the stone for the music made of
wearing away, for the grating roar of wars.
Listen: it's our song.

Darling, dance with me under the moon, hanging
like an onion, hoarding its sugars—sweetness
locked in cells, praying for escape: flames, butter,
breath—a well-honed blade.

II

# Unabashed Sapphics on Hot and Heavy

Exalt the exhale, the doomed plosive of breath.
Tender legislators, permit us love one
last time. Though guts harangue us for food, wafer
of flesh, though throats unslaked

groan for water, wine, let the exit of breath
sustain us, let us run on fumes. The purpling
dark of dawn runs on and on, a spool of red
surrounded by the white

light of gristle, the marble that corrugates
our veins. Listen for the glassy, throbbing hush
that annihilates the need for speech, that dumb
tussle of the tongue

for, for what? Exalt the exhale, screw the need
to take in and in; the Eucharist isn't
all it's cracked up to be. Here I take what you
give up, the real sweet meat

of breath expended, nothing left but a lack,
Babel burning, planks singing into our palms,
some extra syllable we never needed
blessing our starved bodies.

# Sparagmos

*Dionysian rite; the act of rending, mangling*

We're so good at tearing apart        voided
checks, love letters, charred carrion
trapped in a savannah fire eons ago
good gamey god        cooking blew up
our bare-bones brains        because all life
depends on a doom-eager star        something eating
something else        because we gave ourselves
dominion over the makeshift circus
of myth        now we can story as we see
fit        Dionysus had his Bacchae divide
by hand his cousin Pentheus whose own
mom rallied the frenzied throng        we'll do
anything to come together        at communion
a tablet of unleavened bread        I no longer
partake of the dream        Christ's body
in my hands        but I wish I did
a few years back a referee in Brazil
was stoned, quartered, and decapitated
because of a bad call        the fans
at the minor league match piked
his head at the half line
we are expert bread breakers        listen
the disembodied head of an Orphic goat
sings in the dreamy trees tonight        the dead
center of its voice cannot hold        the water
buffalo in *Apocalypse Now* was really
hacked up        remember how it buckled
under the long blades        butter-soft

under the weight      green going
from its aqueous eyes      look
I want to put this all back together
maybe when we awoke the world was whole
what perfect teeth, opposable thumbs
we needed the edible kingdom to fit
in our mouths piecemeal      a great fire
climbed the sky and we came      starving

# Omophagia

*The eating of raw flesh; follows* sparagmos

We power walked through a graveyard
to get to Copenhagen's *best* beef tartare.
Late July, the loitering light smooth-talked
the headstones, the marble tombs, the grass
tamped down over Kierkegaard's grave.
Katerina's legs. Pillars of cypresses.
I know: so many lovers gone to seed,
so much highfalutin light. Breathless
at Manfred's, I stilled my spinning head
against the cellar wall, gulped a glass
of golden Georgian wine. *Are you all right?*
she asked. Yellow marigolds gilded
the plate of minced raw beef. Sweet nothings,
we keep leaving flowers for the dead.

# Meeting *la Matriarca*

Like a rotten habanero
Leila's right big toe weeps in the rust-violet light.
In an unfamiliar home, in the hills above Route 66,
I blot pus still oozing from last night's drunken,
barefooted misstep. She straddles the kitchen sink
and I taste apple in her ankle.
                           Her mother swings
through the backdoor with flank steak, onions,
tomatoes, green bell peppers for *ropa vieja*:
old clothes. Before we even shake hands,
she reduces sugar in water for the flan,
tells me I'm too skinny.
                          Leila decants Tempranillo
into a carafe. We steal glances at the bandaged toe,
though Señora Grau never asks her daughter
*Why* or *How*.
                     I imagine Leila fifteen years ago,
a child sneaking stray ropes of meat between her teeth.
Her mother burns the sugar: *Mierda*. Kneeling twilight
sets motes of dust in amber about us.
                         This woman
who named her daughter after darkness eyes me
as a suspect, suspends me in the lengths of her silences.
I want to say—but don't—that a face passes down
like dusk over foothills, that the meat is so tender
it tastes of someone else's childhood.
                         Señora Grau,
once a child in Havana who fainted awaiting rations
of chocolate, explains that most nights she's too tired
to cook, which is just as well since memory can ruin
a recipe easy as flan.
                     When we've finished eating,
easing in the stewed, caramelized scents of the kitchen,
she tilts her glass in the lamplight, spills a little wine:
"More old clothes, *Flaco*?
                       We also have apples."

# Corazón de Tierra

*Now all I hear are the vines rustling as I go.*
*— Larry Levis*

Red dust rose from the dirt roads
in Valle de Guadalupe like spindrift,
rouging the grape leaves, the olive trees,
the caballeros ambling with donkeys
along the main drag, the air itself.
In a tasting room that towered
over the valley like the altar
of a Mayan temple, wines
from young vines reared
like wild horses on our palates.
Posing as honeymooners,
we spoke broken Spanish
to the women with dark hair
and eyes who flared their wrists
at the end of each pour. They talked
about varietals, terroir, how hard
the grapes in our glasses had to struggle.
We nodded, even understood a little.
We drove the arterial roads all afternoon
with the windows down, hair reddening
with dust. Later, after the sun unburdened
the sky, its afterthought like threads
of saffron on the horizon, we drove
to a restaurant in the body of the valley
called Corazón de Tierra. The waiters
wore starched white shirts, black ties,
and spoke to us as if we were wealthy

Mexicans from Mexico City.
Throughout the evening
cats balanced on moonlit sills,
back from night kills in the vineyards
to stalk around our ankles
for leavings of goat confit,
deconstructed tamales,
oysters from Ensenada.
Lost in the opulence of a vacation
neither of us could afford,
we occasionally held hands across
a table made from wine barrels,
saying things we'd said to others.
But none of that matters.

I only want to illuminate
the ride there, vines shaking in dust,
a boy on the side of the road limping
toward some kind of eternity.
His left leg sluiced a waning river
of blood below torn denim.
Rifted down to the bone,
the wound seemed to crawl
like magma blackening against
the surf of a jagged shoreline.
The boy looked through us
as if we were nothing more
than ankle-deep water,
his leg riveting the road
with each step, stirring up
the fine dust we had washed
from our faces. Still, I drove

to an elegant dinner I've come
to remember with shame,
mouth salivating for Guadalupe's
bracing wine, its ferric dirt roads,
drought-wracked land where I passed
a vagrant boy not yet in his twenties
who will lose his leg and likely
his life in a few days. He'll look
into my eyes but I won't hear
the rustling of vines or the rattle
of the change in his paper cup.
I'll look at his leg and drive on,
the sky one vast raveling of red.

# The Amateur Cook and His Lover

*Eat and love, to be sure, but you better eat first.*
*— Jim Harrison*

She cried over her bowl of carbonara:
no one had ever cooked like that for her.

The egg-laced spaghetti steamed, a soul
singer moaned about the aroma of a woman

no longer his woman, the pendulum
of her hips as she walked out the door.

Candlelight murmured like a nervous heart
as they raised spools of pasta to their lips,

the night melting like sautéed onions. More
Motown women and men crooned warnings

from their smoldering lungs, the songs of loss
a soundtrack for full-bellied sex, how we allow

our bodies to be consumed, lips to fuming ribs,
groins collapsing like black holes in the brain.

But all this is memory, the woman having gone
gluten-free years ago, the man now eating alone.

# Diminishing Sestina

After she said *anorexic,* I wanted
to embody her body, to make her flesh
my flesh, to build us a temple of bread,
a church for us to chew, a faith without
*thou shalt not* and no such thing as weight.
To believe in nothing but appetite.

Ancient, this feigned absence of appetite,
a gibbous moon waning, a lack of want,
the weight of the weight of weight,
the meat and potatoes of flesh
going and going without.
Lucifer wanted a stone turned to bread,

and though we can't live on bread
alone, how we burn with appetite.
No animal can live without
the supreme engine of want,
the brute fact of flesh
awaiting

our teeth. I thought her weight
was okay, didn't notice the bread
always left on her plate, her face flushed
when people said, *You're so petite,*
or when I asked if she wanted
to go out

to eat. From *an* (without)
plus *orexis* (desire). From the weight
we put on the image we each want
to see (the moon proofing like a loaf of bread),
to the advertised appetite
for perfect flesh:

the flesh
without
appetite,
or weight,
or bread,
or wanting.

I used to say, *Bon appétit*, as if our flesh
were blessed with want, as if this weightless
faith would be unto our bodies as bread.

# My Mother and My Father in the Kitchen

Day before my brother's wedding,
the kitchen's humming with dusk,
rusty light like the mottled patina
on the carbon steel blade my father
slips through onions, eyes shimmering.

Beside the sink, brows scrunched,
my mother peels potatoes,
the skins gliding into the trash bin,
the room singing with the swift
raspy tune of honed edges.

And I, who have no memory
of when they were still married,
stand between them, sipping
a bottle of beer, late light trapped
in the glass like ancient amber.

# Grits (and Love and Happiness)

Corn particulates in a thick starch matrix—
porridge basically, a gloopy meal of mush
made from maize, an annual cereal grass
that gave itself out in ears of clockwork
kernels, sweet toothy cells gift-wrapped
in papery husks, the crop so generous
and manifest that the Muskogee called it
*mother.* You wouldn't need a definition
of grits unless you grew up in the smog
and static shine of Los Angeles suburbs,
front lawns stretching below the blades
of palms toward the gilt union of hunger
and convenience, a TV-dinner-loving
stranger to the stable, butter-slicked staple
of southern kitchens. This wasn't supposed
to be about me, but now I'm remembering
"Love and Happiness" by Al Green, a song
my dad used to play in his truck when he'd
pick me up Friday afternoons from the house
he and my mom both used to call home, off
the album, *I'm Still in Love with You*, released
two years before a girl named Mary Woodson
hurled a pot of grits hot enough to melt skin
onto Al's bare back after he said he wouldn't
marry her. Blisters big as chicken eggs bubbled
up before Mary left the room and shot herself
in the head. But I couldn't have known this
then, nodding along in the truck. Couldn't
have known how much I'd grow to love
Motown and the motherly pitch of grits.
I was just a kid en route from one home
to the next, and a song about happiness
stuck to my dad's ribs—the heart of it all
hidden like sustenance in the husk.

# Saying Grace in a Time of Drought

*After Andrew Hudgins*

*I can't believe you danced with HIM!*
one man shouts at another as they stagger
out of the Atlanta Eagle and quarrel
in front of my apartment. I smoke
in the shadows, snooping behind a hedge.
A roach lumbers along a stone wall.
Cicadas click viciously. August,
the city thrums in a thick mug of sweat.
I pray that the lovers can work it out,
go back to grinding in the neon glow.
Inside, my rib eye's roiling in a bath
of butter, blistered garlic, crackling
rosemary, so I leave the lovers
onstage to harangue the night away.
In Old English, hunger means *desire*
*with longing.* So of course, I'm thinking
of a woman who I never thought would
leave, who of course did. Once I awoke to
a roach drowning in the coupe glass she left
on the sill, the insect flailing in boozy,
life-ending ecstasy. Outside, the couple
gnash their teeth, a choked *I fucking*
*love you!* cracking the insect fever pitch.
Too impatient to let it rest, I slice
into the steak, the blood seeps onto
the plate, and I wonder about the ways
we're hardwired for pleasure, how the body
rewards us for outpacing death, the chiasmus

of food and sex. This woman, this woman—
but what's the use in telling you her eyes
had the hard glint of polished obsidian.
That I was the first man to cook a steak
for her. That she'd mouth a silent prayer
over her food like it was God-given.
Now framed by the kitchen window,
the lovers will not, will not stop breaking
up, wringing out their love, overacting
what might be the most important moment
of their lives. Grace, we say, because life
is full of undeserved hunger. The roaches
are out tonight, prowling for crumbs, cracks,
for the sugar in our cocktails. But why bother
telling you? The meat's getting cold.

# Consider the Oyster

*After M. F. K. Fisher*

Their jagged moon faces gaze up at you
from a bed of ice pellets, lemon slices
waiting, alien beside shallot-laced
mignonette. Consider the jagged lips,
the calcified shells, these seafaring fungi.
Born of bracken, born of osteon (Greek
for bone), the ancients grew them on sunken
pottery shards, shucked and slurped over tales
of all-consuming Aphrodite, who
rose from sea-foam, from a womb of silver
nacre, a pearl to make the world burn, god
who gifts us these aphrodisiacs, god
who says it's never about the oyster
but the person eating across from you.

# Quitting

We smoked. We smoked. We smoked one, then another, then another. Our smokes held hands, daisy-chained like lemmings into the abyss. We smoked because of that third drink. We smoked because our conversation was just getting good, because our words needed silver flesh. We waved our smokes like wands, casting love spells over each other. The gossamer architecture of spiders. We made our packs lucky by flipping a single smoke upside down. Saved these for last. We smoked because the body goes on and on and—let's face it—gets bored. We smoked because of the movies. We smoked even though old people smoked: exasperated kayakers drifting toward the waterfall's lip, my grandpa churning lung cinders in a hospital bed. We smoked until, pissed off, I said, *Do you really need another fucking smoke?* We smoked after sex. We smoked before. Ember holes in the sheets. We jaundiced our fingertips with smoke. Inspected the pale, yellow crescents: *How much did you smoke last night?* We smoked while cooking, half in, half out the kitchen. One foot dripping the River Styx. You get the idea. We smoked when Sam Cooke came on. Because he was murdered by a madam in an hourly motel. We smoked because death was just another disappointed parent, a high school principal. We smoked because we were friends, then lovers, then brittle, sexy exes. We smoked because we were already forgiven. We smoked until we couldn't stop. We smoked. We stopped. No. Wait . . .

# Travel Notes: Mykonos

And I remember the octopus salad
our first night on the island.

And I remember the candles flaring
on each table in the crowded taverna.

And I remember children plucking
the feathers of a wayward pelican.

And the beautiful waitress
who pinched their ears, then coaxed
the bird back down the shore.

And I remember saying, after too much
red wine, that dogs are like toddlers,
only more loyal.

And you, then, signing the air
to signal for the check.

After that I remember the ouzo
we drank from the bottle without water
to bridge all that water between us.

And I remember the raw thread
of your long, foreign cigarette.

And your ankles in the Aegean
as ships buoyed in bulbs of light.

And those lights going out
as the stars became legion.

And I remember walking back
to our hotel in the dark, on a road
so narrow I had to walk behind you.

# Japanese Maple

*For Pete Fairchild*

Drinking alone, I studied the tremor
of her bluish hands, the old poet's wife,
each time she raised her martini for more:
the vodka gauzy in the glass, the ice
particulates shimmering like cellar
motes of dust floating in a slant of light.
Her shaking hands, time's unruly decay,
in a bustling bar on Valentine's Day.

The poet looked at her as if she were
a Japanese maple, the leaves burning
burgundy in a breeze, their crisp whisper
drowned out by the boisterous flirting
of twentysomethings sipping liqueurs
like they already knew about love. Sing,
Kansas poet, laureate of the lathe,
the steady blue notes of trembling praise.

But the lights were so low neither could read
the menu, and they both struggled to get
the bartender's attention, their drinks dead
as ragged glaciers. Oh, let them be wet
as rain tonight! Let him butter her bread,
communion plunging a stone into flesh
like there's no tomorrow. Another round,
Kim: their waltzing roots thirst underground.

Though my shift had ended, I had nowhere
better to be. Hypnotized by her hands,
I drank slowly from a mirror of beer,
thinking that it's probably Parkinson's,
that each of our bodies will have an affair
with some cancer or disease, make demands
to cough up our time, whittle us to one.
I closed my eyes. And then they were gone.

# Drinking Her Husband's Rakija

Entombed for over twenty years in the guest room closet,
stowed among photo albums and boxes of souvenirs,

the spirit had been waiting there since her husband's death,
losing its edge, getting bored in the redundant darkness.

Shrouded under layers of plastic wrap, the neck rounded
with rubber bands to prevent evaporation's theft, to keep

time from sneaking sips, the now-brittle bands breaking
into pieces as she unswaddled the unlabeled bottle.

Not made from must, but what's left after making wine:
stems, seeds, skins. *We never wasted nothing*, she said,

filling up our delicate glasses. I repeated her toast—*Živjeli*—
and the spirit's rough heat, mellowed by so much rest,

billowed like a time-lapse rose in my chest. She told me
that my curls reminded her of her husband, Milan, the man

she fled former Yugoslavia with after his older brother,
a priest who loved Bach as much as God, was *assassinated*

*by the communists.* Milan's broad olive face beamed from
the picture frames. A whisper of grapes. A cassette of

Tchaikovsky crackling on her stereo. Under the shine's
spell, we drifted back to the old country, to the Adriatic's

hardscrabble beauty. A small village in Istria where they
killed only one pig a year, where black truffles flourished

in the forest, and dogs were never pets. The home where
her father quietly drank himself to death, having survived

the camps *because he knew how to cook*. I refilled our glasses
in her fully owned New Jersey home, fumes tap-dancing

above the etched bulbs. She spoke of having to give birth
at a refugee camp in Italy, arriving at Ellis Island penniless,

lugging a single suitcase and their strange Slavic tongues.
The symphony ended. When she went to flip the cassette,

I stole another sip, not because I'd heard the story before,
but because I knew what was coming next: hunger like

I have never known, scarcely scraping by with two kids,
year after year trying to make it in America, the city's lights

glittering across the river like innumerable gold teeth,
a few flush years flashing in the maw and pitch, and then

the ellipsis of pinched breaths leading up to Milan's
untimely death: unceremoniously struck by a truck

while out for a jog. I could only nod, knowing nothing
of real loss. Nothing, maybe, except how to praise, how

to keep the glasses full. So we toasted—*Živjeli*—almost
in sync, looking each other square in the watery eye,

me and my grandmother-in-law-to-be, the windows
of our glasses open like the framed face on the wall,

our throats open for the bittersweet business of nothing
in life getting wasted, not the dregs of pomace, nor

the ghosts of nations that no longer exist, every spirit
waiting to be fetched from closets we no longer use.

III

# Renunciation

My shaking hands nicked and slick with blood,
I went to my father with the pocketknife
I'd just got for Christmas and said, like my life
depended on it, *Dad, it's just no good—*
*please get this away from me.* He looked
down at my bloody boy's hands, and I cried
as he must've cried, too, when his wife,
my mom, left him. Renounced her love.

Some thought Sodom and Gomorrah
were green iterations of the garden,
until fire swept the sky like an aurora
and buried two cities in a flat salt bed.

Burning, burning—we hold fire wild and roar:
*Take this gift from us, let there be an end.*

## First Food

In the beginning we ate the words raw.
Like sunlight they lit us up, summering
our skins, deepening belief in the body.
Sometimes, the words told bogus stories,
like the one where I was born—*poof*—
from a rib bone. We nodded, lounging
in tall grasses, watching for eyes in that
dividing blue, waiting for the sweet click
of night so we could finally be ourselves,
speak in our native tongue, that limitless
language of groins. Two teenagers waiting
for grown-ups to leave the house, hungry
for one hot minute. We always knew
we were naked. Light, dark, repeat.
Words shivering in the trees, words
blinding, watching us, words, words,
words, naming every single thing.
*Let there be a little action*, we prayed.
One day, I walked to the tree called
"No" and plucked a soft-bellied bulb
of fruit, nude as the moon, humming
with sun. Hands skittering like leaves,
I ran to my friend with it, and I can't
remember what we said or who bit first
and does it even matter? Like the first
fuck it all came and went so fast, a blur
of luscious flesh roaring over our lips
and down our chins, floating us like red
feathers in a river unraveling to sea,
tongue-tied at the edge and a little

action at last!—the sky dark as a fig
as we dangled above the blue abyss,
the words back at it, thundering
their tantrum of myth. For once, then,
silence. We walked off into the dark.

# For Everything in Paradise

*O Lord Thou pluckest me out*
    — "The Waste Land," T. S. Eliot

Let us not forget it was a behemoth
of fire rushing at a rate of one football
field per second that devoured Paradise.
Let us remember unprecedented, recall
how quickly apocalypse comes for us.
How this pocket of the Sierras went up
like a scherzo. Swift matchstick music.
Like a shrieking chorus of cottonwoods
and a violin section of lodgepole pines—
each needle a celestial cinder, each cell
a cymbal-exploding magnum opus.
Let listening now not be hopeless.
Let us not get carried away dreaming
of Paradise's first residents, those kids
stumbling drunk on figs, their bodies
naked as two flints and the new world
blazing like a pile of pencil shavings.
No, let's remember instead the sound
of the man's voice on the radio after
the roads to Paradise were finally
reopened, home in on the moment
he turned the corner in his pickup
and saw that his house had burned
down, feel the gutturals combusting
as he realized the remains of his wheel-
chair-bound wife rested among the ashes.
Their chimney standing still. Proud as

stone, and lonely as Lucifer. My God,
let us not be plucked out this time,
but imagine the timbre of burning-alive
kestrels hammering their wings as they
tried to flee, birds of prey like papier-
mâché moths. Let our mouths tunnel
the air, choke up on the point-blank O
of horror. Let us someday stand outside
a burning home and say a few words right
to the flames: O fire, how you connected
everything for a few hours in Paradise.
O loose-tongued hunger, barn burner
who chose us of all the creatures
as your apt pupil, your ravished lover
and raw material. Let us abandon all
faith in the ability of metaphor to save
us and say something honest to the man
whose disabled wife perished in a pain
we can't imagine and a Paradise we can
never know: *Let us never know*. Let us
always be plucked safe and stranded
in smoke, grateful for our blackened
lungs. Let us just this once make roar
of your roar, parsing out the bones
in the ashes. Let us hold your words
as you burn our papyrus and melt
the tongue. Let us tell each patient,
unlit candle, that though you wear
the flaming mask of the face of God—
like us, you know not what you do.

# Reckoning

And how, puny poet, would you have me speak?
You repeat and repeat but get nowhere new.
Trace me back as far into the labyrinth
as you'd like, blind beast

with your soft hand on the unraveling leash.
Poor metaphor, expected sword double-edged
but lion-beautiful, gleaming, maw-awful:
breathing, just breathing.

Amanuensis, how could you ever hope
to taste with a febrile tongue the liquid heat
of theodicy, the red-bearded father
of fire-loaded love?

Heave that heavenly gaze into your pupil:
Paradise kindling, pin-prick pines, a whisper
of smoke choked from embers sloughing off ashes
in a far-off hearth.

Abandon your ouroboros, flame-brimming
gyre, circus conflagration, rusted garden
gates, broken crucible: there's no symbol fit
to make me make sense.

Hiding, inflammable, you only cry out:
*There is the whole world and who will put it out?*
Unsung, the once-wild, ghost-green earth goes on
screaming in my mouth.

# Butter Thief

*Enoch walked with God; then he was no more, for God took him.*
— *Genesis 5:24*

In an etched-glass tomb, in the frail fire of dusk, a stick of butter
softened on the linen-draped table. Adults waltzed around

the kitchen with cocktails, the ice in their glasses of whisky
whispering into liquid. Pre-Deluge, Enoch ate the birds

of the air, the fishes of the sea, all beasts. The world rocked
itself out of the womb, keeled over into a land of grasses lush

with the slashes of a brother's blood. I crawled on my hands
and knees, snuck up to the linen-draped table, carefully lifted

the lid of the crystal sepulcher, and swiped a thick fingerful,
letting the fat become oil and the oil become otherworldly

on my tongue. I was told Enoch was plucked from the earth
because he was so good. After the butter, I touched a shining

stack of *Playboy*s in my grandpa's bathroom, the light vacant
in its westward descent, a slow melt across the horizon's skillet

toward a distant cradle of haze called *Los Angeles*, and an ocean
called *the Pacific*. Like most miracles, butter was an accident:

a goat-skin bladder filled with milk bumping along the saddle
of a horse until the cream converted into something more solid

than the sum of its parts. Once, I tiptoed the kitchen, God-fearing
thief of the flesh's fat riches. I could have been taken any second.

# A Lesson in Hunger

*For Chris Abani*

He told us by candlelight of his imprisonment.
Our circle of twelve shadowed faces followed
the arc of his accent as it lilted over words like
*coup, torture, Nigerian guards, tough motha-fuckas.*
The tin serving tray—a kaleidoscope of braised meats,
red lentils, collard greens, fiery refrains of *berbere*—
swiveled into stillness, and the spongy folds of *injera*
lay like linen under our palms. He told us about
solitary, the firing squad. Looking into a rifle barrel
like a bottomless well of water. He spent two weeks
starving, accepting the death penalty so the classmates
who acted in his satire could go free. He only paused
to stir or sip his Americano, breath spaces like rings
widening around a skipped stone. Most of the time,
I can imitate nothing but the artifacts of communion,
render nothing worth enduring. *The finer things in life*
echoes like a knife-struck wineglass, and I hear jazz.
He told us of the ransom his family paid, his sojourn
in the UK. He published a book of poems about Kirikiri
Maximum Security; days later assassins stabbed
to death an African neighbor. He said beware
of omens. He said this was the best Ethiopian
in Los Angeles. After his story we tore at the bread
soaked with pepper butter and filled our mouths
with the immediacy of feasting—our only response
to devour the food he treated us to, to turn our faces
toward each other by degrees, each of us sent
like the tray in orbit of a stewed center.
In the afterlife, if there is a just God,
I'll repay each meal I ate without hunger.

# Varieties of Communion

*After* The Vulture and the Little Girl *(1993) by Kevin Carter*

Dear Lord, allow me to say that it's not
about hunger, thirst, or a plump vulture
patient as a tombstone: the way of nature.
Not the girl, more crossed than Christ, caught
in the photographer's frame, a green knot
of spare grass growing around her finger.
Not ekphrasis, privilege, or aperture.
Not this damn image I thought I'd forgot.

No matter what you captured, Kevin, I hope
it wasn't guilt that made you kill yourself.
Maybe you saw that we'll all be as bread
torn and scattered in the desert, our bones
bright manna abiding the soil, the self,
burnished in the shade of a starving bird.

# After the Last Supper

This isn't about Leonardo's brushstrokes,
the tempera pigments destined to decay
on the convent's plaster wall, the remains
restored so many times even the ghosts
of the original—the stunned apostles
gesticulating, the glasses of thin wine—
have all gone down the gullet of time,
never to return, regardless of gospel.
This isn't about the vanishing point
at Christ's right temple, how our eyes
funnel into focus where the image dies
and comes back to life, his airy mind
the fulcrum of the flaking simulacra.
This isn't about twelve men arguing
about betrayal, each refusing to bear
the weight of blame, unable to begin
to understand what's at stake, bread
and wine hereafter fixed as ephemeral
sacraments, body and blood of a guy
who dies believing he's been abandoned.
No, this is about the woman (she must
have been a woman) who hobbled out
of the kitchen to clean up the aftermath
of a feast for zealots. Picture her stacking
dirty plates, empty cups, not caring about
the rim that touched his lips, or the hard,
half-eaten loaf he held aloft as if it were
miraculous. It's late and she's too tired
to worry about the fate of these guests.
Thousands of last suppers exist and she

is in none of them, patient saint sweating
in the ash-darkened kitchen, bowlegged
and paying dogged attention to a simple
herring stew, or the ascension of water
and flour into bread. Let the fanatics
go on babbling at the crowded table.
This is about those who make manna
sing behind the scenes and stick around
to sweep after the ritual has ended.
Flesh converted back into crumbs,
spilled salt, the almost invisible
filaments of fish bones. Forgettable
table wine fading to vinegar.

# Whenever You Eat This

*A bakery was also struck, killing at least a half-dozen people
lined up for bread.*
— The New York Times, *Aleppo, 2016*

Breath, manna, body of God,
leavened alchemy of yeasts,
primordial slow-boiling dough,

trinity of water, flour, and salt,
fermented, fired, an image of air,
crust like a child's scabbed elbows—

we reach for you over porcelain,
across ironed linen, fisted loaves
flowing from swaddling baskets.

We open our refrigerator doors
for paper-white slices machine-beaten
into iron-fortified eucharists,

choosing these bleached logs
over the gnarled, scored flesh
that was surely Christ's bread.

Ethereal, whole, you're ancient
inheritance from the Crescent,
vital as a mother's breast.

Breads of the last bakery in Aleppo—
*Khubz arabi, lavash, saj, chubab*—
our tongues lean toward you.

But we've witnessed nothing,
never seen a grandmother bent
by scoliosis scoop up a scrap

of salty fallen bread, then bless
it with her lips, amen, and take it
into the furnace of her body.

Life itself, holy glutenous spirit,
did the bakers sense something off
as they skipped you, sponge soft

into the blistering brick ovens,
their hands grasping the callused
handles of their heirloom peels—

did they know it, dear gift from God,
and did the war-weary, stomach-shrunk
martyrs waiting in line for this, their daily—

did they all understand that this morning
still becoming morning, beginning to rise—
that this would be bread forever awaited?

Tell me, did the flames render them
supernatural, other, borne of breath,
spirits unshackled of flesh, no longer

bolted by bones? In that last flash,
in the hail of glass, brick, and shrapnel,
did they ascend like seraphim

riding fire toward the light?
No, sour father, omnipresent
yeast, they must've been more

humble, more human than that,
smote like the charred sunspots
on a perfectly baked wheel of pita.

# Bethesda

Jesus snuck in through the sheepgate
to get to the pool of Bethesda.

In this retelling, the sky reels with twilight,
and the pool burns the colors of fire.

A paraplegic junkie waits on his mat for angels
to eddy the water, for the miraculous tremor.

Jesus and the junkie talk under the fire
of the sky, beside the placid sheet of water.

Hobos moan, beat the air with palm fronds,
their eyes fixed doggedly on the water.

The junkie complains that no one will dunk him
when the angels begin their frenzied swimming.

Jesus says, *Man, forget about the water.*
Two kingfishers scribble across the sky,

painting the pool's surface in streaks,
teal wings teasing like water over flames.

*Forget it, huh?* The paraplegic gets up and laughs,
leaves as all the beggars of Bethesda shudder.

Jesus saunters off against the golden hour,
silhouette backlit, no less, no more, than myth.

In this rendition, I believe the story of Bethesda.
In others, I lie down and moan beside the water.

## Jesus as a Jaded Lover

I gave my body and what you gave me
was coffee and burnt toast in the morning,
love poems, prayers that cried, *Me, Me, Me.*

What a wild night! You couldn't believe
your moonlit luck, thunder-relieved longing—
I gave what you could never give to me.

You cut panes of stained glass so I could see
inside your church, but the crowds were yawning;
your love poems only babbled, *Me, Me, Me.*

Wow, man. Don't you get it? I set you free
from thirst, my sweat a fine red wine pouring
from my body. What did you give me?

A fumbling one-night stand, a lame story
of ecstasy you'll ache remembering
in one-sided prayers, bad poems about me.

And now this purling verse, about to be
dust, deleted, uneaten. Look baby,
I gave my body burning. All you gave
were poems, prayers: less than air to me.

# Miracle in a Time of Dregs

*A malfunction causes red wine to flow from faucets in an*
*Italian town.*
              *— CNN, March 2020*

No less numinous than blood leaking
from the marble eyes of Mary, opened
from a slow birth of stone, stone feigning

breath, a woman, a crafted conception
no less miraculous than virgin birth:
the sculptor's imitative petition.

In the end, what will it all have been worth,
the statues weeping honey, the milk—
the far-flung faiths of the Podunk earth?

I would've got drunk with Jesus and his ilk,
the wedding at Cana suddenly lit, a rager
after he spiked the water, a thing like ink

blooming the brain's blank pages. Players
of the play's penultimate act, the people
of Castelvetro, locked in like the layers

of an onion, saw their sinks fill and ripple
with fizzy, ready-to-drink Lambrusco,
red providence they poured into bottles,

praising the faulty plumbing. Keats also
prayed for a reason to sing, for a *draught*
*of vintage* to drain his stone-sober sorrows

to the dregs. We too need odes to outlast
this dry season, a sea of wine-dark belief
purpling our lips and teeth until the last

galling call. No less luminous are these
our doom-eager days. Dog days we have
to sing, and to believe before we leave.

# Saying Grace in a Time of Too Much
### (Elegy for a Future Loss)

After us, Lord, that kudzu's a-coming.
A great green wave's gonna feast on our graves,
flood the highways, get blind-drunk and glutted
on our scratches in the dirt. It was good
for a while though, shacked up in our lovers'
mesh tent, loose, on the lam, the blood-hungry

mosquitoes knocking, the veggies hungry
to swallow us up. End time's a-coming.
The bloodhounds out for murderous lovers.
After us, the whole world one long lush grave,
vines for veins, and no one to say it's good,
our throats compost, flowers for gutturals.

Flashes of eloquence, we knelt, gutted
trout by streams, saying gilt-tongued grace, hungry
as animals, as Bible salesmen. Good
Lord, like wildfire that green's a-coming!
Coming for to carry us to our graves,
the fallow field, the seed's long-lost lover.

I tried for elegy, my basil-eyed love,
to be read the night you leave me gutted,
my fat tomato heart fallen, a grave
man indeed. The burning world's hungry
for us to leave, for that ever-coming
canopy, that raw, all-consuming god.

Honey, apocalypse ain't the end. Good
endings swing a scythe, unearth new lovers,
buried gardens. Nature's knight's a-coming,
riding our own fire right toward us, glutted
on butter and bourbon and gas, hungry
to save his beloved, lay us in our graves.

God, let us bless the earth with our graves,
make marigolds bloom from bone dust, make good
of our grand Gomorrah days. How hungry
have we been? A moody, mismatched lover
who refuses to give up, dream glutted
on tomorrow, flesh forever a-coming.

Lord, let us still be hungry in our graves.
Let what's a-coming come for good, the earth
its own beloved, glutted after we're gone.

# Saint Prodigal

These days, the talk's about return.
Not the glorious hog-wild years
on the road, my ritual worship
of rib joints, Coke cups of beer,

women you don't bring home.
I miss the blue smoke of a blues
riff mixing with the hard smoke
of oak and a sweet sooey muse.

Now they say I'm a miracle,
bona fide, a lucky cap that made
its way back from the lost and found,
a dog who knows how to stay.

Of course, my brother threw a fit
when he saw me show up shoeless:
he knew I gamed it, planned to be
bailed out all along and blessed

with Daddy's best beloved calf.
A homecoming feast for the son
whose most prodigious sin is
feasting, a belly never done.

Forgive me, friends, for I regret
nothing, no knuckle of butter
or slab of fatback, my body's
cast-iron debt to pleasure.

So what if I crawled back broke,
and begging and raw to the bone?
My tank is full, and I just wrote
the pigs—I best be getting home.

# Revelation

To begin with rapture and leave you in
a matter of seconds, the world yet to be
finished, like wine lingering on the lees,
or yeast slowly coaxing flour to leaven.

To be less than a grain of salt, crystalline
zip in the simmering sea. To be steadily
wearing away despite this blessed daily
breaking of bodies. To see that we begin

with our need to eat. To be a heathen
and be done with it. To leave irony
at the door and split before the party
ends. To write a book of revelation

sans pale horses, lakes of sulfur and blood.
To go down chewing, and know that it's good.

Gregory Emilio is a poet and food writer from southern California. His poems and essays have appeared in *Best New Poets*, *Gastronomica*, *North American Review*, *[PANK]*, the *Rumpus*, *Tupelo Quarterly*, and *Southern Humanities Review*. He holds an  MFA from the University of California Riverside, and a PhD in English from Georgia State University. A mean home cook and avid cyclist, he lives in Atlanta and teaches at Kennesaw State University.

# ALSO FROM ABLE MUSE PRESS

Jacob M. Appel, *The Cynic in Extremis: Poems*

William Baer, *Times Square and Other Stories; New Jersey Noir: A Novel; New Jersey Noir (Cape May): A Novel; New Jersey Noir (Barnegat Light): A Novel*

Lee Harlin Bahan, *A Year of Mourning: Sonnets (Petrarch): Translation; Advent and Lent: Sestinas and Sonnets (Petrarch): Translation*

Melissa Balmain, *Walking in on People (Able Muse Book Award for Poetry)*

Ben Berman, *Strange Borderlands: Poems; Figuring in the Figure: Poems; Writing While Parenting: Essays*

David Berman, *Progressions of the Mind: Poems*

Lorna Knowles Blake, *Green Hill (Able Muse Book Award for Poetry)*

Michael Cantor, *Life in the Second Circle: Poems*

Catherine Chandler, *Lines of Flight: Poems*

William Conelly, *Uncontested Grounds: Poems*

Maryann Corbett, *Credo for the Checkout Line in Winter: Poems; Street View: Poems; In Code: Poems*

Will Cordeiro, *Trap Street (Able Muse Book Award for Poetry)*

Brian Culhane, *Remembering Lethe: Poems*

John Philip Drury, *Sea Level Rising: Poems; The Teller's Cage: Poems*

Josh Dugat, *Great and Small: Poems*

Rhina P. Espaillat, *And After All: Poems*

Anna M. Evans, *Under Dark Waters: Surviving the* Titanic: *Poems*

Nicole Caruso Garcia, *Oxblood: Poems*

Stephen Gibson, *Frida Kahlo in Fort Lauderdale: Poems*

Amy Glynn, *Romance Language (Able Muse Book Award for Poetry)*

D. R. Goodman, *Greed: A Confession: Poems*

Carrie Green, *Studies of Familiar Birds: Poems*

Margaret Ann Griffiths, *Grasshopper: The Poetry of M A Griffiths*

Janis Harrington, *How to Cut a Woman in Half: Poems*

Katie Hartsock, *Bed of Impatiens: Poems; Wolf Trees: Poems*

Elise Hempel, *Second Rain: Poems*

Jan D. Hodge, *Taking Shape: Carmina figurata; The Bard & Scheherazade Keep Company: Poems; Finesse: Verse and Anagram*

Stephen Kampa, *World Too Loud to Hear: Poems*

Ellen Kaufman, *House Music: Poems; Double-Parked, with Tosca: Poems*

Len Krisak, *Say What You Will (Able Muse Book Award for Poetry)*

Emily Leithauser, *The Borrowed World (Able Muse Book Award for Poetry)*

Hailey Leithauser, *Saint Worm: Poems*

Carol Light, *Heaven from Steam: Poems*

Kate Light, *Character Shoes: Poems*

April Lindner, *This Bed Our Bodies Shaped: Poems*

David Livewell, *Pass and Stow: Poems*

Susan McLean, *Daylight Losing Time: Poems*

Martin McGovern, *Bad Fame: Poems*

Jeredith Merrin, *Cup: Poems*

Richard Moore, *Selected Poems; The Rule That Liberates: An Expanded Edition: Selected Essays*

Richard Newman, *All the Wasted Beauty of the World: Poems*

Alfred Nicol, *Animal Psalms: Poems*

Deirdre O'Connor, *The Cupped Field (Able Muse Book Award for Poetry)*

Frank Osen, *Virtue, Big as Sin (Able Muse Book Award for Poetry)*

Alexander Pepple (Editor), *Able Muse Anthology;*
    *Able Muse: A Review of Poetry, Prose & Art* (semiannual, winter 2010 on)

James Pollock, *Sailing to Babylon: Poems*

Aaron Poochigian, *The Cosmic Purr: Poems; Manhattanite (Able Muse Book Award for Poetry)*

Tatiana Forero Puerta, *Cleaning the Ghost Room: Poems*

Jennifer Reeser, *Indigenous: Poems; Strong Feather: Poems*

John Ridland, *Sir Gawain and the Green Knight (Anonymous): Translation;*
    *Pearl (Anonymous): Translation*

Kelly Rowe, *Rise above the River (Able Muse Book Award for Poetry)*

Stephen Scaer, *Pumpkin Chucking: Poems*

Hollis Seamon, *Corporeality: Stories*

Ed Shacklee, *The Blind Loon: A Bestiary*

Carrie Shipers, *Cause for Concern (Able Muse Book Award for Poetry)*

Gabriel Spera, *Twisted Pairs: Poems*

Matthew Buckley Smith, *Dirge for an Imaginary World (Able Muse Book Award for Poetry)*

Susan de Sola, *Frozen Charlotte: Poems*

Barbara Ellen Sorensen, *Compositions of the Dead Playing Flutes: Poems*

Rebecca Starks, *Time Is Always Now: Poems; Fetch, Muse: Poems*

Sally Thomas, *Motherland: Poems*

Paulette Demers Turco (Editor), *The Powow River Poets Anthology II*

Rosemerry Wahtola Trommer, *Naked for Tea: Poems*

Wendy Videlock, *Nevertheless: Poems; The Dark Gnu and Other Poems;*
    *Slingshots and Love Plums: Poems; Wise to the West: Poems*

Richard Wakefield, *A Vertical Mile: Poems; Terminal Park: Poems*

Gail White, *Asperity Street: Poems*

Chelsea Woodard, *Vellum: Poems*

Rob Wright, *Last Wishes: Poems*

Printed in the USA
CPSIA information can be obtained
at www.ICGtesting.com
JSHW080919170923
48379JS00004B/108